P9-BZQ-523

DATE DUE

HOW MANY TEETH?

by Paul Showers   illustrated by True Kelley

Revised Edition

HarperCollins*Publishers*

Let's-Read-and-Find-Out Science is a registered trademark of
HarperCollins Publishers.

How Many Teeth?
Copyright © 1962, 1991 by Paul Showers
Illustrations copyright © 1991 by True Kelley
All rights reserved. No part of this book may be used or reproduced
in any manner whatsoever without written permission except in the
case of brief quotations embodied in critical articles and reviews.
Printed in the United States of America. For information address
HarperCollins Children's Books, a division of HarperCollins Publishers,
10 East 53rd Street, New York, NY 10022.
Typography by Andrew Rhodes

Library of Congress Cataloging-in-Publication Data
Showers, Paul.
   How many teeth? / by Paul Showers ; illustrated by True Kelley. —
Rev. ed.
      p.   cm. — (Let's-read-and-find-out science. Stage 1)
   Summary: Introduces teeth, describing how many we have at various
stages of life, why they fall out, and what they do.
   ISBN 0-06-021633-6. — ISBN 0-06-021634-4 (lib. bdg.)
   ISBN 0-06-445098-8 (pbk.)
   1. Teeth—Juvenile literature.   [1. Teeth.]   I. Kelley, True, ill.
II. Title.   III. Series.
QP88.6.S56   1991   89-13995
612.3'11—dc20   CIP
                                                                      AC

Revised Edition

HOW MANY TEETH?

4

Here is Paul.

He is a new baby.

He has no teeth.

He does not need them.

He drinks milk and orange juice.

How many teeth has Paul?

He has no teeth at all.

He drinks his breakfast and his dinner, too.

He doesn't need teeth to help him chew.

Very young babies never do.

Here is Elizabeth.

She is not a new baby.

She is one year old.

She has six teeth—four upper teeth
and two lower teeth.
Elizabeth needs teeth to help her eat.
She likes to bite things with her teeth.

Elizabeth likes to bite.

She does it from morning till night.

She bites her food and her teething ring.

She tries out her teeth on everything.

She bites her cap.

She bites her sweater.

She would bite the cat's tail if he would let her.

Babies with teeth like to bite.

11

This is Sam.

He is Elizabeth's brother.

Sam is a big boy. He goes to school.

Every day he goes to school with his friends
Larry and Tom and Lucy, Sandy and Mary and Bill.

Sam has twenty teeth.
He has ten upper teeth
and ten lower teeth.

14

His front teeth have sharp edges.

He uses them to bite things.

His back teeth are flat.

He uses them to chew things.

Most of Sam's friends have twenty teeth—
ten upper teeth and ten lower teeth.

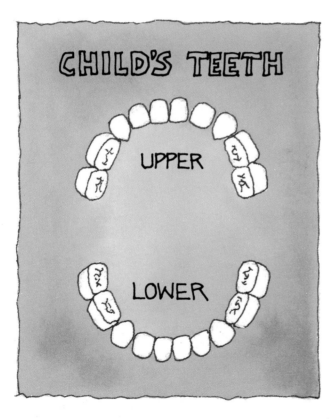

How many teeth to bite and chew?
Sam has twenty teeth;
Larry has twenty teeth;
Sandy and Lucy and Mary
have twenty teeth.
How many teeth have you?

This is Sam's father.

He is bigger than Sam and he has more teeth.

He has thirty-two teeth.

He has sixteen upper teeth
and sixteen lower teeth.

UPPER

ADULT'S TEETH

LOWER

18

This is Sam's mother.
She has thirty-two teeth.
Grown-up people
   need a lot of teeth.
They have sharp teeth to
   bite their food.
They have flat teeth to
   crush and chew their food.

19

Thirty-two teeth
for biting and crushing.
Thirty-two teeth
need a lot of brushing.

20

Sam has a loose front tooth.

He wiggles it with his toothbrush.

He wiggles it with his finger.

He wiggles it with his tongue.

It feels good to wiggle it.

A new tooth is growing under that loose tooth.

The new tooth keeps pushing.

That makes the old tooth loose.

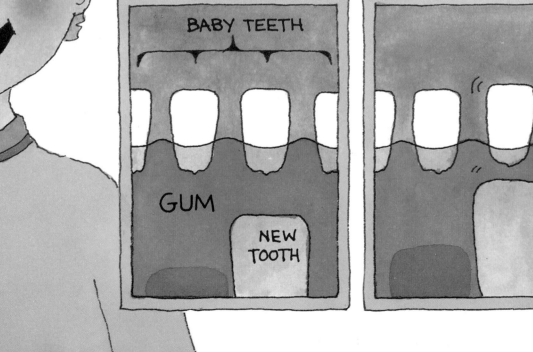

BABY TEETH

GUM

NEW TOOTH

Soon the old tooth will fall out.

Then there will be room for the new tooth.

The new tooth will be bigger than the old one.

Out go the old teeth;
in come the new.
Sam needs bigger teeth
to bite with and chew.

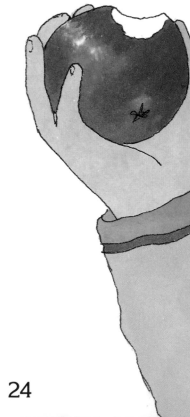

Sam is growing up.

He is getting his grown-up teeth.

He will have them for a long, long time.

Sam brushes his teeth every night.

He brushes them every morning.

He takes good care of his new teeth.

He will keep his new teeth for the rest of his life.

Out go the old teeth;
in come the new.
Sam is growing up,
and so are you.

Many of Sam's friends have loose teeth.

Lucy can wiggle her lower front tooth.

Sandy's upper tooth is very loose.

Soon it will fall out.

Maybe it will fall out tomorrow.

Lunch
Tom Bill
Sam
milk

Sandy
Lucy

Tom
Bill

Sam and his friends made up this verse.
Read it out loud.

How many teeth has a baby?
How many teeth have you?
Oh, Sam has a loose tooth;
Sandy has a loose tooth;
Lucy has a loose tooth, too.

Bill cannot say the verse very well.

Do you know why?

Because two of his teeth came out.

When he smiles, he looks like this.

When he tries to say the verse, it sounds like this:

> How many teeth hath a baby?
> How many teeth have you?
>   Oh, Tham hath a looth tooth;
>   Thandy hath a looth tooth;
>   Luthy hath a looth tooth, too.

And he can't wait to get his new teeth.